HOUSTON

Designed and Produced by

Ted Smart & David Gibbon

MAYFLOWER BOOKS · NEW YORK CITY

Introduction

IT has become a cliche to call any city with a cluster of modern buildings in its center the 'city of the future.' Many such cities, though possessing new skyscrapers, are built within the accepted traditional terms of reference of the "city": an urban area with a center in which commerce and entertainment are concentrated and which is the focal point of city life.

Houston, though it has a major concentration of tall buildings at its heart, does not fall into the traditional concept and, by not doing so, it breaks completely from the historical character of cities as places that offer centralized protection to their inhabitants and communication to its business people.

Houston is a sprawling city of many centers, each of which is self-sufficient in its services and entertainments and whose shopping malls, protected from the weather, are interconnected by tunnels that make it possible to move from one to the other without leaving the protection of the whole complex. The various centers are connected by freeways giving easy access to each other and freeing Houstonians from the inconvenience and discomforts of urban public transport.

With its explosive development in the past two decades Houston has been able to embody many of the ideas of modern planners without the problems facing cities that have developed from existing urban communities. There have been few old buildings to demolish or to protect and there has been no resistance from residents to the horizontal development of residential estates. The city has therefore developed as a vast homogenous community whose arteries are the freeways and whose life beats in the great complexes of buildings such as those at Greenway Plaza or Galleria.

At the beginning of the century Houston was a quiet little Texas town of some half-million inhabitants, its means of livelihood being the export of cotton, and the produce of the ranches that stretched into the interior. In 1901 oil was discovered at Spindletop Field near Beaumont and changed Houston's destiny. This was the spark that ignited the population explosion that is making the city one of the most populous on earth.

The really big upsurge in population did not begin until World War II, when Houston's oil and oil-derived industries became of paramount importance. During the war years more and more industries were developed and the port of Houston thrived, becoming one of the major ports in the United States. After World War II a census revealed that Houston and its surrounding districts had increased from three hundred thousand inhabitants in the 1930s to six hundred thousand. Today the population of Houston is over two and a half million.

Greater Houston incorporates four areas: City of Houston, Harris County, Houston Standard Metropolitan area and Houston Galveston Standard Consolidated. Overall the four areas cover nearly 17,000 square miles with the city itself occupying 507.64 square miles. The population of the whole area is nearly seven million.

The city is situated along Buffalo Bayou, a tributary of the San Jacinto River which flows into Galveston Bay along the shores of the Gulf of Mexico. It bears little resemblance to the early trading post of Harrisburg, which was the earliest inhabited sector and now is located on the southeast side of modern Houston.

The first impression of Houston is of a vast urban area of low-built houses spreading across the prairie and defined by an arabesque of freeways that curl around the city center and spin off in all directions like the arms of a Catherine Wheel. To the north lie Austin and Dallas, to the west San Antonio, to the east Beaumont and to the south Galveston.

In the heart of this great city are the skyscrapers, tall and sheer, gleaming in the southern sunshine like the silos of the craft whose journeys into space are plotted at the NASA command base on the southern fringe of Houston.

Around the tall buildings are large open spaces where neatly parked rows of automobiles reveal the method preferred by Houstonians for getting to and from work. Some of the spaces are plazas and parks; others are building sites awaiting the development of some new architectural complex.

Downtown Houston is essentially a place where people work and is inhabited around the clock mostly by visitors who come from all over the United States and most of the countries of the world, either on business or pleasure, and they stay at the vast hotels that dominate the city center. Other arrivals are those who have been attracted by the promise of good jobs and opportunities in the booming city. There are 40,000 newcomers every year and they are responsible for a growth rate that is double that of any other U.S. city.

In the early days of the city's development the indiscriminate building of dwellings and the pressures of a sudden increase in population produced the usual urban problems of crime, pollution and urban sprawl; a legacy which the present city administrators are still struggling with though much work is being done in the control of city planning and community services to improve the quality of Houston life.

Early pictures of Houston show a typical American town with wooden buildings in which the Gothic style prevails or those solid stone edifices reminiscent of the architecture of Medicean Italy. A very different scene from the one that the visitor to Houston today encounters. Not everything has changed, however, and thanks to the enterprise of some of Houston's citizens a little of the past has been preserved. Much of this is around the Market Square where the old City Hall, which was turned into a

Across Sam Houston Park the massive skyscrapers tower beneath a cloudless sky pages 4 & 5, while by night pages 10 & 11 the city is transformed by a million glittering lights.

Houston's elaborate road-system left curves round the city like a gigantic meccano set.

bus station, still dominates the surrounding area where restaurants and cafés remain as a reminder that this was the place where saloons and women entertained the Saturday night out-of-town visitors.

From the period of the Twenties, when the oil business made fortunes overnight and the money flowed as fast as the black gold, there is the Rice Hotel, still a splendid building and reflecting its former glory though it has been extensively modernized. Already in this period some half a million automobiles circulated in the city and caused traffic jams in Main Street, which led out into the country and the new airport opened in 1928. This was the period of bobbed hair, the Charleston and Howard Hughes, Sr., who was laying down the foundations of the great Hughes empire later inherited by his son.

Many of the buildings of the Twenties have been replaced by the tall downtown skyscrapers of today; one of the most recent is the fifty-story One Shell Plaza which was the work of Gerald D. Hines, one of the most active developers in the city. One Shell Plaza, which has a smaller sister named Two Shell Plaza, rises between Smith and Louisiana. Not far away is another fine example of Houston's advanced architecture, the Pennzoil building with its twin trapezoid towers, also by Gerald D. Hines. Pennzoil Place is constructed of glass and steel and is a complex of two buildings separated by a narrow ten-foot gap with a sloping roof which joins the buildings at a steep angle up to the eighth floor and provides shelter for the plaza area below.

A striking feature of downtown Houston is the miles of tunnels that link up the complexes of shops, restaurants, plazas and malls that form the center of the sprawling amoeba-like city. In these interlinked complexes Houstonians could, if they wished, live without the need to venture out into the open streets and in this cocooned existence they are free of the usual metropolitan aggravations of traffic and polluted air as well as the vagaries of the weather.

Outside the central downtown city ringed by its inner circle of freeways the houses stretch out toward the distant horizon, the low-built urban architecture punctuated here and there by a cluster of high-rise blocks denoting a shopping or entertainment center. One of the largest of these lies to the west along the South West Freeway. This is the Post Oak Plaza Shopping center and the Galleria. This was also the work of Gerald D. Hines and consists of an impressive group of buildings including the luxury Houston Oaks Hotel, a theater, restaurants and even a skating rink.

Nearer to the center of Houston is the Greenway Plaza, a 127-acre complex with office buildings, hotel, sports arena, blocks of apartments and an underground shopping and parking concourse.

Altogether there are some dozen of these self-contained centers of shopping and entertainment scattered about the Houston urban spread.

Within the Freeway Loop that circles around the city immediately by the downtown skyscrapers are some of the most important city features: the museums, universities, medical center, sports palaces and so on. All of them are well endowed and like everything Texan aim to be the best, if not the biggest, of their kind.

The museums of art are plentiful and thanks to the lively Houstonian interest in a past with which they have few connections there have been purchases of important and rare European works of art to enrich the galleries. Furthermore, much of the culture of which Houston is justifiably proud is the result of patronage by citizens whose wealth has been the product of Houston industry.

A tribute to the importance of oil in the development of Houston is paid at the Museum of Natural Sciences, where a Hall is dedicated to the subject of oil and its exploration and use.

Activities linked to the space exploration program have also created new fields of experimentation. One of these is in medicine, where Houston leads the world, particularly in the area of heart surgery and cancer research.

The Houston Medical Center that lies to the south of downtown Houston is one of the finest in the U.S. It is also one of the most innovative. Within its buildings there are hospitals, colleges of pharmacy, schools of public health and many other services. Nearby lie the wooded acres of Hermann Park.

Near the medical center lies Rice University which provides for nearly four thousand students. Thousands more attend the University of Houston and Texas Southern University, both campuses of which lie to the west of Rice University along the Gulf Freeway.

Hermann Park faces Rice University and is one of the most attractive open spaces in Houston. There are 545 acres of it, presented to the city by George Hermann in 1914, and they include playgrounds, a theater, a planetarium and a zoo.

In the park's rose garden there are 3000 plants of 100 different varieties, and the Camellia Garden is famous for its many species of this sweet smelling flower which is so characteristic of the southern states of America. There is also a garden designed for its fragrance and though not designed specifically with blind people in mind, the garden gives them as much pleasure as those who are able to see it.

One of the principal children's amusements in Hermann Park is the Santa Fe and Texas Chief, a train, which in the course of its two-mile journey, takes its passengers through hills, forests and along lakes crowded with wild fowl.

Another and larger park is Memorial Park to the west of the city on what was once a training ground for World War I soldiers. The park includes a golf club, a tennis center, a polo ground, sports fields and botanical gardens. The botanical gardens are filled with trees and the indigenous flora and fauna of the bayou. There are 250 acres of them with walking trails that are popular at weekends with Houstonians who are able to walk through a countryside which has changed little since the pioneer days and contains a great deal of Texas wildlife including, unfortunately the Bayou mosquitoes.

The Memorial Park is the scene of one of the great events of the Houston year: the Rodeo and Livestock Show. Though rodeos are part of the regular entertainment in Houston the one that takes place in February and March is exceptional. Traditionally most participants ride into the city along the old cattle trails with their evocative names like Old Spanish Trail, Prairie View Trail, and Texas Independence Trail. The riders gather in the Memorial

Park the evening before the parade and there is all the atmosphere of old cattle camps to create the mood for the following day. In the morning as many as 6000 horses and wagons set off downtown for the big parade along Main Street and Travis to the accompaniment of bands led by majorettes and the cheers of spectators. The cowboy costumes and the horses' harness are more Hollywood than genuine pioneer style but this all adds to the colorful procession.

The parade is the opening event of two weeks of nostalgia for the good old days and there is a livestock show, wild bronc riding, bull riding and all the heroic pursuits that have become the legendary attributes of the Texas cowboys. The size of the bulls as well as the hogs in the show is evidence of the improvement in breeding methods, since the first ranches were set up and the skills of the riders owes as much to the modern scientific approach to sport as to the natural talent of the riders; nevertheless the fun is fast and furious and exciting.

The rodeo takes place in the Astrodome, a Houston landmark in the world of sport which Houstonians like to call the eighth wonder of the world. Situated on the South Loop Freeway the Astrodome makes spectating a sybaritic pastime, for one can drive into the air conditioned arena, glide up to a seat on an escalator, and sit in an artificial atmosphere without the normal aggravation of cold, wind and rain that most sport-watching entails.

There is room for 66,000 spectators in the stadium and they are kept informed of the progress of the game, and also encouraged to give vent to their enthusiasm, by a vast electronic system, which includes a two-million-dollar scoreboard.

Those who yearn for the conventional style of sport-watching can go to the Rice Stadium at Rice University. This is also a vast place and although it lacks the electronic gadgetry of Astrodome, the excitement of watching a game of football or baseball in company with other fans is no less lively than in the stadium where every comfort is provided.

Opposite the Astrodome lies another form of entertainment, which is thriving in the cities of America at the present time; this is a vast amusement park named Astroworld. In Astroworld the visitor can undergo a variety of experiences on the one hundred rides that the park offers; between the gentle rocking of swings and roundabouts to the violent shaking up provided by the roller coaster there is every conceivable kind of system of locomotion including a sleigh ride over an Alpine run, and a journey on the 6.0 Limited.

There are 260 municipal parks in Houston covering an area of 5,747 acres and these are scattered about the greater city and the surrounding counties. Many of the parks have sporting facilities including golf clubs, tennis centers, swimming pools and football and baseball fields.

In Harris County there are plenty of opportunities for sailing and fishing on lakes, the best-known of which are Sylvan Beach and Clear Lake Park to the south of the city.

Houston is joined to its port by a ship canal, a sixty-mile-long waterway which opens up the city to the world's shipping lanes and has been indispensable to its growth and development. When the idea of a city on Buffalo Bayou was first put forward by the Allen Brothers the canal was nothing more than a vegetation-choked waterway which small boats could navigate with extreme difficulty. By 1960 Houston's port had become the third largest port in the U.S. In 1977, Houston moved over one hundred million short tons of cargo, half of which was for foreign trade to such countries as Japan and Saudi Arabia.

The canal joining Houston to the sea has a ship basin at the Houston end only four miles from the city center and its depth of 40 feet and width of 400 feet allows the passage of ships of considerable size. From Houston port some 120 shipping lines provide service to all parts of the world.

In addition there is a network of canals that links Houston to waterways in the Mississippi basin and to other southern canals. These provide a cheap form of transport for goods to and from inland cities which are also served by six major rail systems.

Houston's two airports, the newer Intercontinental and older William P. Hobby have gained international importance with services to more than twenty foreign airports throughout the world.

To keep this fast moving, explosively growing city under control Houston has a mayor-council government. The City Council is composed of a mayor and eight councilmen and is responsible for local legislation. Three councilmen are elected from the whole electorate and the other five represent specific districts. Elections take place on odd number years. Most of Houston is situated in Harris County which is governed by Commissioners Court, consisting of four commissioners and a county judge. The court is an administrative body responsible for the law and civil administration.

Houston's development and design, with its decentralized center and its freeway communications, should be able to assimilate the increasing population drawn to it from other parts of the country as well as from abroad. That the numbers will continue to arrive seems inevitable, for Houston is a boom town with plentiful natural resources and room to expand. The climate is agreeable, mild in winter and hot in summer, though it tends to have a high degree of humidity. Houstonians escape from it to the beaches along the coast at Galveston, Bolivar Peninsula and Freeport.

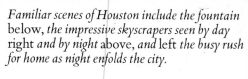

Familiar scenes of Houston include the fountain below, *the impressive skyscrapers seen by day* right *and by night* above, *and* left *the busy rush for home as night enfolds the city.*

The view overleaf *clearly indicates Houston's development potential.*

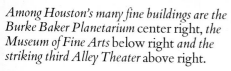

Among Houston's many fine buildings are the *Burke Baker Planetarium* center right, *the Museum of Fine Arts* below right *and the striking third Alley Theater* above right.

The sleek lines of the city's modern edifices can be seen bottom center, in the Houston Center Buildings 1 and 2 above, and left, in the innovative glass and steel towers of Pennzoil Place.

Below *is shown one of the exhibits in the Contemporary Arts Museum, while overleaf is featured the skyline of Downtown Houston.*

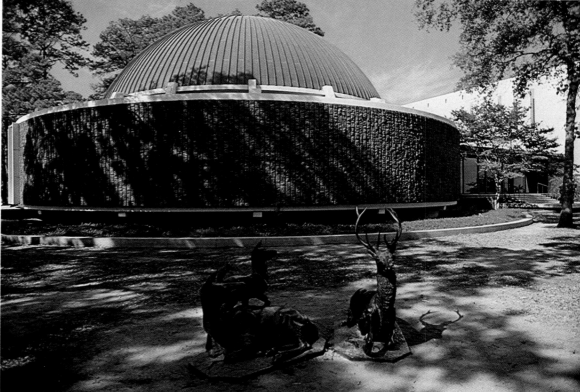

Houston contains a wealth of diverse architectural styles admirably illustrated on these pages: *the Hyatt Regency Hotel* above far left, *the Kellogg Building at Greenway Plaza* below far left, *the Contemporary Arts Museum* below left, *the Neurosensory Center and Cullen Eye Institute* above left *and the cluster of modern buildings, including the Sheraton Hotel* above right. *The gracious Warwick Hotel is shown* below, bottom *the Cotton Exchange,* above *the Nichols-Rice-Cherry House* and right *the Church of San Antonio.*

Downtown Houston is seen overleaf *across tranquil Sam Houston Park.*

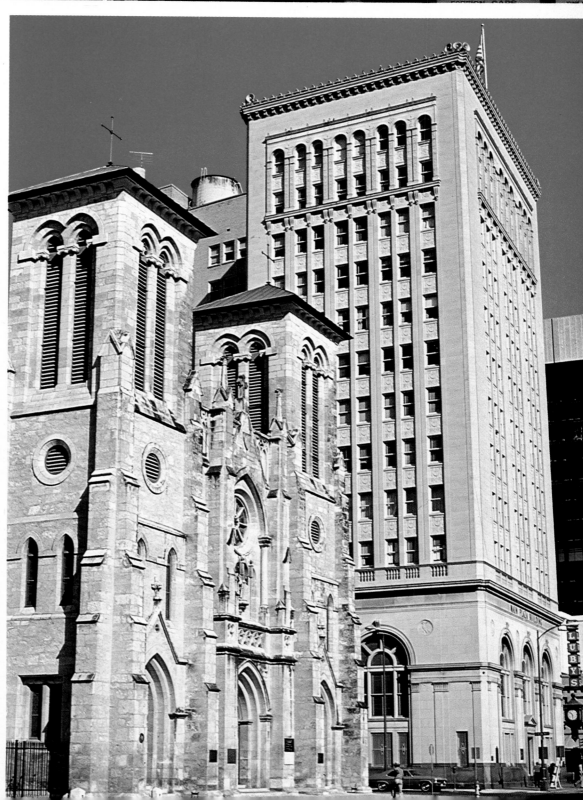

The History of Houston

IN the early days of the nineteenth century a rider watering his horse at Buffalo Bayou on the Brazos River would have been hard put to imagine that one day a great city would arise in the swampy mosquito-ridden shores of the stream around which grew a jungle-like vegetation. There were few settlements in those days, only trading posts set up by the French, Spaniards or Americans who roamed the Southwest of America looking for trading opportunities, including those in the slave business.

It was the Austins, father and son, who first saw the possibility of setting up permanent colonies in what was later to be Texas. Moses Austin obtained permission from the Spanish Governor of San Antonio as a result of his friendship with Felipe Enrique Neri, who interceded on his behalf—and for the first 300 Americans and English – to set up homes between the Brazos River and the Colorado. The work of Moses Austin was carried on by his son Stephen and later by others who began to see the immense possibilities of this vast new land.

The Brazos River flowing down to Galveston had a special attraction for the new colonists; it provided a link with the sea, though getting boats up and down through the thick vegetation along its banks was an arduous business, and it flowed through a fertile valley where crops would grow well in the Southern sunshine. Soon a village was founded by John Richardson Harris and it was appropriately named Harrisburg.

Sensing the future danger to their sovereignty the Mexicans, who had won independence from Spain in 1821, began to put difficulties in the way of American immigration and the tension that ensued came to a head when the Mexicans began to impose heavy import dues on the settlers. Two Americans, De Witt Clinton Harris and Andrew Briscoe, were imprisoned at Anahuac and this led to the formation of a vigilante group to free the prisoners and throw out the Mexicans. When William Barret Travis arrived with a cannon on the sloop *Ohio* and fired it at the jail, victory was complete, with the Mexicans fleeing from the customs post which was promptly occupied by the Americans.

The ignominious retreat by the Mexicans hardened the attitude of their government under General Santa Ana and orders for the arrest of Travis were posted while Santa Ana himself moved with his army to teach the rebels a lesson. Meanwhile the settlers had themselves decided on forming their own force, and defying the Mexicans, they named Sam Houston its chief. It was a ragged collection of troops but they were all of them tough and intrepid frontiersmen. Two hundred of them including Davy Crockett, James Bowie and Travis waited for Santa Ana at the Alamo.

The outcome of that battle is history. Santa Ana with his superior forces overwhelmed the Alamo and pursued the refugees across the country, but at Harrisburg a resolute band of citizens of the new Texas Republic dug themselves in. In the meantime there had been much activity on Galveston Island where vessels arrived carrying supplies for the rebels. These supplies were moved upriver to Harrisburg on which Sam Houston and his hard pressed force were retreating.

Santa Ana arrived first, but found a deserted village, all the inhabitants having fled at his approach except for the editor of the *Telegraph and Texas Register*. Setting fire to the town Santa Ana retired to await reinforcements. At this point Sam Houston arrived on the scene with his small force but with two cannons which had been presented to Texas by the city of Cincinnati.

Houston had less than 800 men to Santa Ana's 1400 but he had cannons and his men had not acquired the Mexican habit of taking a siesta. Choosing his moment, Houston launched an attack in the heat of the afternoon moving his men quietly through the grass until they were within a quick dash to the stockades. The cannons then opened fire and within minutes the walls were down and Houston's men were overpowering the surprised and panic-stricken Mexicans. In barely a quarter of an hour the battle was over and Mexican domination in Texas had come to an end.

A few months after the battle of San Jacinto the brothers Allen, a pair of enterprising land developers, were advertising the sale of real estate in the new town of Houston. The town existed only in their imagination but such was their enthusiastic description of it that people from all over the country began to move down to Houston, persuaded by the Allen Brothers' word picture of the healthy climate, the navigable river and the fact that Houston was destined to become the seat of the government of Texas.

For a while Houston was a boom town. Then came a blow which crippled its development for decades. The center of government was moved to Austin. Now came a difficult period with yellow fever epidemics, loss of trade and new attacks from the Mexicans. In 1845 however, just as Sam Houston was about to invade Mexico, Texas became part of the United States.

Statehood did not have an immediate effect on the development of Houston but it did provide that stability and security which made a measured growth possible and brought the law and order which encouraged the arrival of new families of settlers. Most of these arrived on the railways that were offering cheap trips in the fifties and their numbers formed the core of a new community of tradesmen and clerks who helped to establish Houston as a sound commercial city.

When the Civil War broke out Houston joined in on the Confederate side with enthusiasm; bodies of guards and rifle companies were formed rapidly and the famous Texas Rangers prepared for action. The effect of the war was more economic than military however. The federal army blockaded Texas by occupying Galveston Island, though this was captured later by General Magruder. When the war ended, many people fearing occupation by the federal troops, left Houston and much of the commerce which had suffered the effects of war was slow to recover.

As the century progressed Houston began to prosper once more, the channel, which made it possible for large vessels to sail right up to Houston, was planned, and new industries settled in the town that was now growing into a city. The new turning point came in 1901 when oil was discovered at Spindletop Field. The rush that followed was like those of people in search of gold, in San Francisco, some sixty years earlier. Fortunes were made and lost as people put their life savings into land which often did not fulfill the buyers' expectations.

On the eve of World War I Houston had grown to over 100,000 inhabitants and the ship canal joining it to its port had been finished and was big enough to take the freighters that carried away the cotton and the products of the ranches that were still Houston's main source of revenue.

Two wars and the growing demand for petroleum changed the destiny of Houston as the century progressed and to these, new sources of wealth were added from the industries that grew up around space exploration.

Today Houston is the world's energy center as well as the headquarters of space exploration. It is not too wild a boast to claim that it is a city of the future whose fate is also the fate of the western world.

The Old Sweeney Clock left, *which dates back to the turn of the century, once fronted the original Sweeney Jewelry Store before being moved to its present location.*

Houston is justifiably proud of its Texas Medical Center shown on these pages, *which was developed to provide the best in hospitalization, research, and in training programs for doctors, nurses and dentists. Within the two hundred acre site is the splendid Hermann Hospital* center left, *which is sited on the Outer Belt.*

Freeway 59 overleaf, *part of the city's vast and complex road system, snakes its way through the metropolis.*

Many of Houston's educational institutions have marvellous sporting facilities, including the Rice University which boasts a fine stadium seen here and overleaf. Captured in these photographs is the exciting football game between the Rice 'Owls', in blue strip and the S.M.U. in red. The 'Owls' mascot is shown below, and left the denim-clad 'Mob' Band entertains during the interval.

Houston, Texas and the World

HOUSTON is the largest city in Texas, its most important port, and plays the lead role in the life of the biggest state in the United States. Though not the state capital, an honor which was transferred to Austin in 1838, Houston is the acknowledged commercial capital and as such it reflects closely the character and life of the state as a whole.

Like the rest of Texas, the city of Houston is populated largely by Texas-born people, nearly 80 percent of whom are white, with 20 percent black and a scattering of other races. Of the whites, 10 percent are Mexican or of Spanish descent. Compared to the rest of the state Houston has a higher proportion of black and Mexican people and is, broadly speaking, more cosmopolitan, like most major cities of international status. Most of the Europeans in Houston come from Britain, Germany, Scandinavia, Poland, Czechoslovakia and Italy and many of them are temporary residents who have business connections with the city.

The population mix and its historical evolution is responsible for the character of Texans and their particular lifestyle. This can be identified in the famed Texan hospitality which is traditionally effusive and big-handed and, on the other side of the coin, in Texan insularity, which creates a barrier between whites and people of other colors. In Houston these traditional Texan traits are less strong, largely because city dwellers inevitably become less individual and also more tolerant as a result of the propinquity of city life.

What is true of Houston also applies to other Texas cities like Dallas, which follows Houston in size though not in industrial activity, San Antonio, a historical city and site of the Alamo, El Paso, a tourist town on the Mexican border, and Austin, the state capital, though in San Antonio and El Paso a higher percentage of Mexican Americans gives these cities a character different from the others.

In terms of the Texas economy Houston leads the way in industry, while in the rest of the state the traditional raising of beef cattle continues to be one of the main industries. Almost 8.5 percent of the land area of Texas is given over to agriculture. Cotton, which was one of the mainstays of nineteenth-century farming, is still an important crop, and grain, fruit and peanut farming are some of the other products of the Texas farms which today, with more mechanized and scientific methods are increasing their yield. Much of the agricultural production of Texas passes through the port of Houston, where it is shipped to other parts of the United States or to foreign countries.

By far the most important product of mining activity in the state is petroleum, with the major fields lying in the eastern part of the state. The industry is based in Houston, where other petroleum-based industries have developed.

Outside of the oil refining and petrochemical industries Texas has a considerable food processing and canning business which has developed since World War II, and tourism now attracts some 20 million visitors a year.

Until recently, the main tourist attractions have been in the towns such as El Paso and San Antonio, which have preserved Spanish and Mexican characteristics. Here the American visitor has found the architecture of another culture, and its music and food as well. To the American people Mexico has the same exotic charm that Mediterranean countries possess for northern Europeans. In their colorful atmosphere, the product of the mingling of Indian and Spanish cultures, the American people of European descent are at ease with the extroverted exuberance and emotional excitement which prevails.

Now the tourists come from overseas and the attractions for them are different. Though the legends of the Old West still stir them they are more likely to be intrigued by the Texas of the future, the Texas that is the world's energy center and the control point of space flights.

The new motive that tourists have found in visiting Houston has helped to make the city better known throughout the world. It has come alive through the reports and writings of the people to whom it has played host, in the same way as other great cities have become familiar to millions of people over the years as a result of the tourists who have stayed in them.

Houston is still a very young city, however. It has the dynamism and the vitality of a place that is in the ferment of creation. Here and there a visitor notices embryonic signs of a new species of city; a kind of vast amorphous residential community with service centers where the inhabitants work and play linked together by the twisting tentacles of the freeways. But the visitor may well wonder if he is seeing the birth of a new planned concept of urban living or merely the frenetic development of a city where free enterprise is allowed unbridled license.

There are signs that the city leaders are waking up to the possible dangers of too rapid a growth with too little control. The Houston phenomenon may therefore be subject to some changes in the next decade but whatever they are they are likely to continue to cause the same absorbed interest and amazement in the world as Houston does today.

Established as a Junior college in 1927, Houston University attained senior status in 1934 and by the early sixties had become a fully state-supported institution. The courtyard of the Student Union at the University is shown right.

Included in the extensive facilities at the 545 acre Hermann Park shown below left are golf, a garden center, the lake seen above left, a miniature train and the Museum of Natural Science and Planetarium.

Houston University is pictured below, and right and above the campus of Rice University, one of the nation's most important educational centers.

The vast Memorial Park overleaf exists on the site of Camp Logan, which was an emergency training ground for soldiers during the latter period of the First World War. The Park includes a golf course and polo ground among its many fine facilities.

Houston offers a wide variety of excellent department and specialty stores, such as Joske's *right* which has a fine range of quality apparel, gifts and furniture and Sakowitz's *below*, renowned for its stylish fashions and giftware; while elegant boutiques, like Isabel Gerhart's *left*, sell chic clothes to be worn perhaps at the Ritz *above*.

One of the city's most popular nightspots is the Great Caruso *overleaf*. Recreated as an Old World opera house, this spectacular restaurant is decorated with fine antiques, and in addition to its acclaimed Continental cuisine offers customers continuous entertainment from classical opera to Broadway favorites.

DISCO

Stephen Burrows

The Lyndon B. Johnson Space Center

THE NASA Space Center has stimulated the business growth of Houston more than any other enterprise, apart from the petroleum industry. More than 3,600 people work at the Center itself and another 6,000 are employed by contractors in the Houston area. This has given a boost to the housing, shopping centers, hotels and educational establishments that are supported by the $1,750,000 earned by the people connected with the Center.

The Space Center has also made Houston world-famous, for it was here that the first moon landing was broadcast to the world, which heard the first words spoken by man on the moon: "Houston. Tranquility Base here. The eagle has landed."

Lyndon B. Johnson Space Center, usually abbreviated to JSC, was built on a 1,620-acre site twenty-five miles to the southeast of the center of Houston. Construction began in 1961 and was completed in 1963. From then until 1969, when the first moon landing took place, the center played an important part in the NASA development program.

The by-products of the enormous national effort to put an American on the moon ahead of the Russians were many, both in the fields of materials and equipment and in the life sciences. Today, those products are still evolving and becoming available to the public. Among them are micro-electronic elements for radio and television, ovenware that will withstand sudden changes of temperature, fire-retarding paints, stronger polyurethane plastics, minute blood pressure and heart monitoring systems that can be inserted in the body by a hypodermic needle without surgery, space food adaptations that provide easily prepared foods for the elderly and the invalid, and many other products.

For the visitor to Houston, the focus of attraction at JSC is the Mission Control Center, from where, seconds after the launch at Cape Kennedy, the first manned space flights were controlled. Today the Mission Operations Control Room is silent, the rows of consoles are unmanned, and the large display screens empty. But that aura which fills historic buildings in which great events have taken place remains to stimulate the imaginative visitor to recall the action on July 20, 1969, when the first astronauts landed on the moon and the voice of Neil Armstrong announced the successful culmination of eight years of total dedication to the mission.

Even more dramatic was the flight of Apollo 13 which was rescued when an oxygen tank exploded when the spacecraft was 200,000 miles from Earth. On this occasion the astronauts had to move into the lunar module for the return journey while the systems on the faulty command module were powered down. The success with which the rescue was conducted and the meticulous hour-by-hour control of the cliff-hanging operation proved the effectiveness of the Mission Operations Control systems at Houston.

These systems were carried out by three basic groups: mission command and control, systems operations, and flight dynamics, all working in the Mission Operations Control, MOCR or Moker, Center. Around them are other support rooms where data on the mission is analyzed and monitored, and where Meteorology, the Lunar Surface, and Recovery Operations are the subject of study by teams of specialists.

For the JSC, one of the most important of all operations was to keep track of, and communicate with, the spacecraft once they had been launched. A tracking and communication system called Manned Space Flight Network was developed. Though this is centered in Maryland the call sign for Mission Control is Houston, and it was this call sign that has remained as the first word recorded by man on the moon.

Though manned space flights and moon shots are not on the JSC program at present there are other NASA projects that are using the resources created for the manned space flights. One of these is the Space Shuttle.

The Shuttle will usher in an entirely new era in space travel and the Lyndon B. Johnson Center at Houston is responsible for the development, production and delivery of the Orbiter spacecraft concerned in the project that will shape a new destiny for mankind. Orbiter is a manned aerospace vehicle designed to carry heavy loads into Earth orbit but it lands like an aircraft. The crew control launch, orbital maneuvering, re-entry into the Earth's atmosphere and landing. Seating for passengers is on a lower deck and there will be little of the discomfort suffered by the first astronauts, for maximum gravity load has been reduced to 3g (three times the force of gravity) during launch and only 1.5g on re-entry. The air-conditioned cabin will be at normal sea-level atmosphere.

Initially the Space Shuttle will have a number of other useful functions which will extend the existing possibilities of space flight. Interplanetary spacecraft can be put into orbit by the Shuttle which will carry them in a payload bay. Once released, the rocket spacecraft can move into a higher orbit or interplanetary trajectories. Similarly, an unmanned space telescope, or even a complete scientific laboratory, "Spacelab," in which scientists can conduct experiments in medical, manufacturing and other fields, can be put into orbit.

Regular runs of the Space Shuttle are planned for 1980 and they will mark the beginning of a space age for ordinary travelers, which until now has only been the subject of science fiction. With Space Shuttle the world will be shrunk even further and a flight across America that now takes five hours will be accomplished in eight minutes!

At Houston this world of the future has already arrived, for the work to make it a reality had been going on for years as anyone who visits the JSC can verify.

The name of Houston is famed throughout the world for its vital role in the U.S. Space Travel Program. A model shown right wears the necessary clothing and equipment for survival in space.

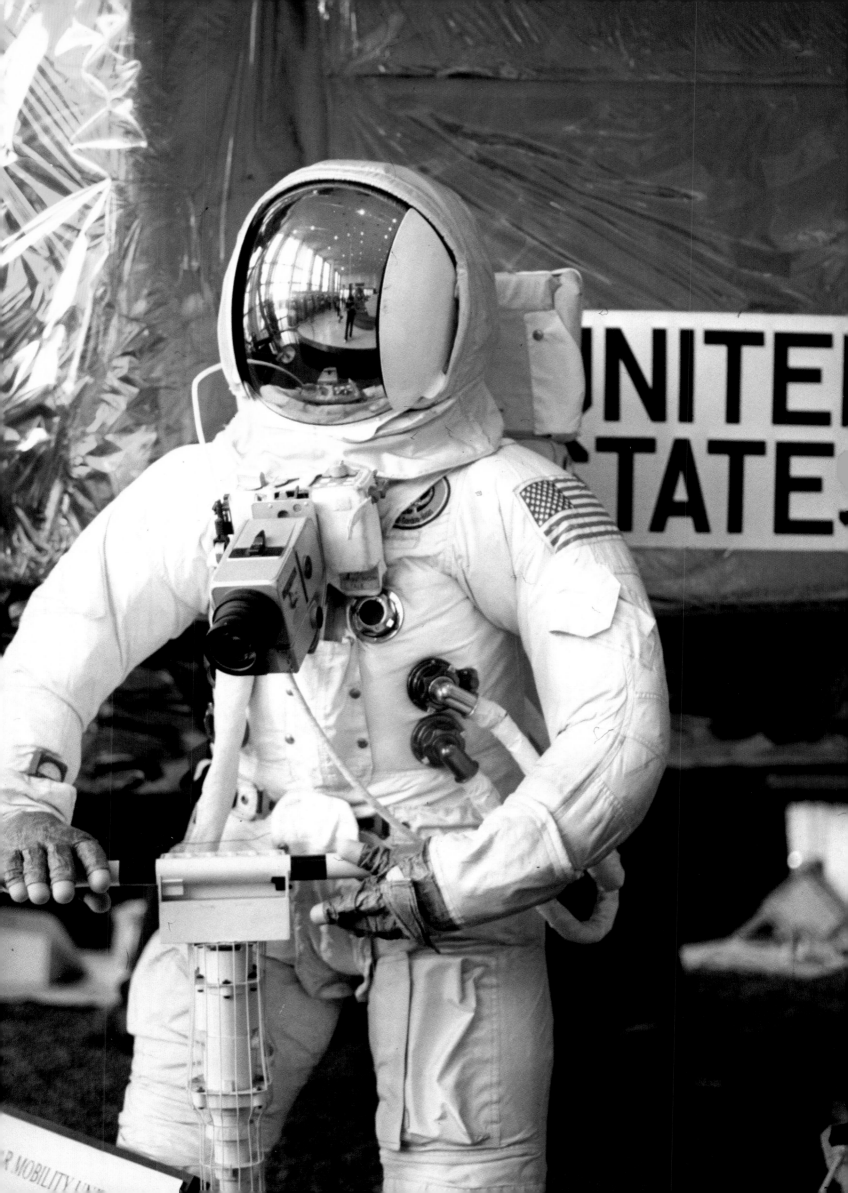

The NASA Lyndon B. Johnson Space Center *above* is situated near Clear Lake on a 1,620 acre site and consists of about 100 different buildings, including the nine story Project Management Building *below*. One of the newest and largest research and development facilities, the center is a focal point of the Nation's manned space flight program. Among the exhibits on view to the public are the Apollo 17 Command Module *far right,* the Travehicular Mobility Unit *right,* the Lunar Module Test Article *left* and the flight articles *above left.*

Some of the most historically significant photographs ever taken, including the Apollo 11 moon landing, are featured *overleaf.*

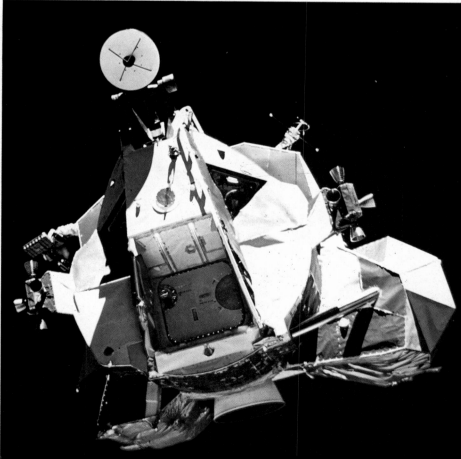

The Galleria illustrated on these pages is a giant enclosed multi-story shopping, office and entertainment complex which features a superb ice-rink shown right. Created by Gerald D. Hines, in the tradition of the market places of old, the Galleria sparkles under its extravagant European glass-domed ceiling, with porticoed shops, art galleries and furniture stores lining its spacious balconies. Visitors to the Galleria can shop, dine and be entertained in a relaxed and informal atmosphere.

Simply furnished, plush or elegant, Houston's fine variety of restaurants offer both excellent cuisine and service. Traditional English fare is a particular attraction at the Red Lion Restaurant top center and above right, while at Foulard's above the specialty is authentic French cuisine. Candlelit dinners are a feature of the intimate Maxim's Wine Cellar Bar right, which is contrasted with the 'bright lights' atmosphere at Annabelles in the Galleria Plaza Hotel below. The beautifully furnished élan Club is shown left, and above left the Bowery Restaurant.

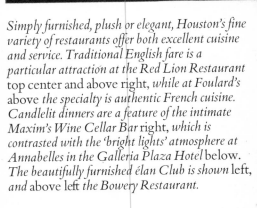

The superbly embellished interior of Courtlandt's one of Houston's most elegant restaurants, is shown left, and above The Window Box in the Hyatt Regency Hotel, where imaginative lighting enhances the decor.

For Italian food Rudi's Restaurant, in the Post Oak below, is well worth a visit and right is pictured a dining-room in the popular Maxim's Restaurant.

The Economic Success Story

IF one must choose a milestone for the start of Houston's phenomenal business success it would have to be the opening of the Port of Houston in 1914. Without its port Houston would have remained a small town, far away from the Eastern centers of wealth and cut off from the rest of the world. The port opened up Houston, making it the center from which the products of the South could be exported and which would attract trade from other countries.

Timber, cattle grain, minerals and cotton were among the important resources that Houston shipped abroad in the early years of the century and, most important of all, oil and its by-products.

Oil was the second milestone in Houston's success, and as the use of oil and the development of oil-related industries increased, so did the importance of Houston.

But Houston was not simply a supplier of raw materials to the industries using the raw materials with which it was so well endowed. From timber grew a considerable manufacture of plywoods, paper milling and furniture-making; from the cattle that were raised by the thousands in the vast Texas ranches developed a highly skilled cattle-rearing business, which has produced some of the fine breeds of Brahman and Charolais cattle.

Mineral production and exploration gave rise to ancillary industries manufacturing the tools required for mineral extraction and the scientific institutions that concern themselves with various aspects of mineralogy. Today the extraction of minerals occupies a large number of the Houston population and among the minerals produced are: sulfur, which comes from the Houston-Gulf Coast, lime from shells and limestone found along the coast, salt, magnesium, which is taken from the water at Freeport and barite, bromine, cements and gypsum from various places in the eight Houston counties.

In 1977 the manufacturing companies in Houston were employing nearly 200,000 members of the working population and Houston had risen to be the world's petroleum refining capital with a total production of over four million barrels of refined products per day.

Houston had also established itself as a leader in the chemical and petrochemical industries and processed 50 percent of the nation's synthetic rubber.

Twenty-nine of the world's thirty largest U.S. oil companies, including Shell, Exxon, Tenneco, Mobil and Gulf have management activities in Houston and four hundred other world companies also have Houston offices. Some of them such as Exxon, Shell and Pennzoil have erected the skyscrapers that dramatize the Houston skyline.

Houston is the leading manufacturer of equipment for the oil industry and many of the companies that produce it have been in Houston since the pioneer days of oil exploration. The most famous of them all is perhaps the Hughes Tool Company. This was founded by Howard Robard Hughes, Sr., who, having struck oil in the first days of Spindletop, set about solving the problem of penetrating hard rock formations when drilling for oil. His invention was the rotary rock bit drill. Its success was instantaneous and the business grew, with other types of equipment being added to the drill. In 1924 Hughes Senior died and left his business to his son Howard Hughes Junior, whose involvement with the aircraft and film industries brought him world fame while his eccentricities gave him international notoriety.

Along with the tool business grew others that produced fluids to facilitate the work of the drills. At the same time there grew a demand for pipelines to carry the oil from the fields to reservoirs and docks, and further requirements were for tank cars, seagoing tankers and offshore rigs. Most of these industries required financing and this gave rise to the Houston banking business which now ranks among the first ten in the U.S.

There are eight Houston banks with international departments and over thirty representatives of foreign banks. The commercial importance of Houston is also recognized internationally by the 47 nations that keep consulates in the city.

Foreign investment in Houston is also increasing and is estimated at several hundred million. The investment has come from governments and individuals from Britain, Canada, West Germany and Mexico and has gone into office tower blocks, apartments, shopping centers, etc. It is only natural that among the nations seeking to do business in Houston many of them should also be in the oil business, thus the Arab nations have strong links with the city which handles over 65 percent of all sales to the Arabs.

The business activity and the large number of visitors in the city have fostered the hotels and catering business, which is up to international standards, and it has encouraged the establishment of shops that sell every conceivable item. Two of the largest department stores are Sakowitz and Foley's. The former was founded in the 1890s and is still operated by the Sakowitz family. Foley's, which is also situated in Main Street, is a ten-story building covering some 735,000 square feet. On Thanksgiving day the store arranges a parade which stretches for two miles with floats, balloons, and bands and has been a traditional event in Houston for the last twenty-five years.

The success of the city and its established position as a center of the energy business attracts many business people to it, many of whom come on business conventions which are held at the modern Houston hotels or at the various convention facilities available in the Civic Center, the Astrohall, the Sam Houston Coliseum and the Summit in Greenway Plaza. In 1977 there were no less than 319 major conventions and the total number of delegates registered at hotels and other establishments was over half a million.

Moored at San Jacinto since 1948, the U.S.S. Texas left and below left overleaf is the sole survivor of the Dreadnought class and a veteran of two world wars.

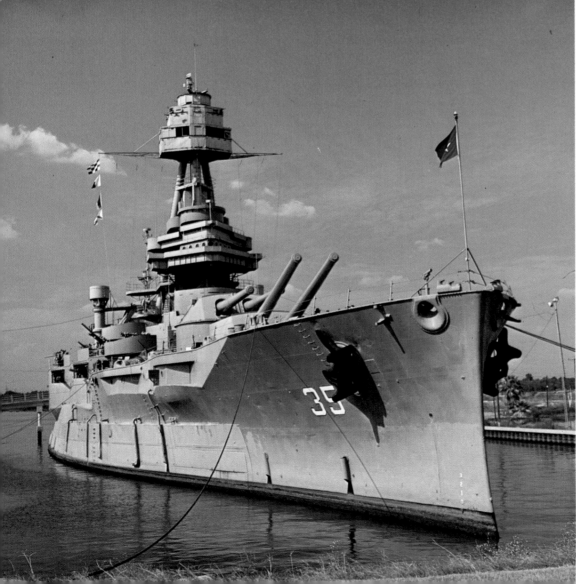

Once just a stream running through the city center, the Buffalo Bayou has been dredged and widened to make the Port of Houston above one of the newest and most modern major ports in the world. Although the port was officially opened by President Wilson in 1914, it was not until the following year that the first regularly scheduled steamship service was started by the S.S. Satilla. Today this bustling port handles international cargoes from all over the world and it is estimated that in an average year almost 5,000 ships, handling about 90 million tons of cargo, will call at the Port of Houston.

DE ZAVALA PLAZA

NAME HONORS LORENZO DE ZAVALA, VICE PRESIDENT OF REPUBLIC OF TEXAS (AD INTERIM, MARCH 17–OCT. 17, 1836).

BORN IN YUCATAN AND EDUCATED IN THE SEMINARY OF ILDEFONSO, DE ZAVALA WAS AN ARDENT LIBERAL WHO WAS JAILED 1814–1817 FOR POLITICAL ACTIVITIES. IN PRISON HE LEARNED ENGLISH AND BECAME A MEDICAL DOCTOR. IN 1821 HE WAS A MEMBER OF THE CORTES IN MADRID, SPAIN, AND LATER WAS GOVERNOR OF A PROVINCE OF MEXICO.

AFTER MEXICO WON INDEPENDENCE FROM SPAIN, HE KEPT WORKING FOR DEMOCRATIC REFORMS. LOYAL TO THE 1824 CONSTITUTION OF MEXICO, HE OPPOSED DICTATOR SANTA ANNA, AND MOVED TO TEXAS TO SEEK FREEDOM. ON MARCH 2, 1836, HE SIGNED TEXAS' DECLARATION OF INDEPENDENCE. LATER HE SIGNED THE REPUBLIC OF TEXAS CONSTITUTION.

MARRIED TWICE, HE HAD SIX CHILDREN. THE FAMILY HONORED HIS MEMORY BY KEEPING ALIVE HIS IDEALS AFTER HIS EARLY DEATH. THE LEGISLATURE OF TEXAS IN 1858 NAMED ZAVALA COUNTY IN HIS HONOR.

LORENZO DE ZAVALA, MANY OF HIS DESCENDANTS, AND SOME OF THEIR NEIGHBORS AND FRIENDS WERE INTERRED IN THE DE ZAVALA FAMILY CEMETERY, ON THE PLANTATION ACROSS BUFFALO BAYOU FROM THIS SITE. THIS PLAZA IS DEDICATED TO THE MEMORY OF VICE PRESIDENT DE ZAVALA, HIS FAMILY, AND OTHERS BURIED IN DE ZAVALA CEMETERY.

(SEE OPPOSITE MARKER)

The famous San Jacinto Battleground above, a State Park covering almost five-hundred-acres, was the site of the decisive battle between Texas and Mexican armies on the 21st April, 1836 which was to secure independence for Texas. Led by General Sam Houston, the Texans, in the eighteen minute battle, quickly secured victory; 630 Mexicans are believed to have died, 208 were wounded and the remainder taken prisoner, while casualties on the Texas side were slight.

Within the area the bronze memorial right and the Monument below left commemorate the heroes of the Battle and all those who helped to win independence for Texas. Constructed in 1936-39, the Monument towers 570 feet high and is built of reinforced concrete faced with Texas fossilized buff limestone. At its base, which forms the museum, are eight massive panels, one of which is shown below, and these are engraved with a brief account of the revolutionary battle.

A road bridge spans the wharf-lined ship channel in the port area overleaf.

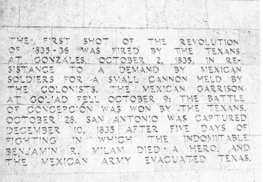

THE FIRST SHOT OF THE REVOLUTION OF 1835-36 WAS FIRED BY THE TEXANS AT GONZALES, OCTOBER 2, 1835, IN RESISTANCE TO A DEMAND BY MEXICAN SOLDIERS FOR A SMALL CANNON HELD BY THE COLONISTS. THE MEXICAN GARRISON AT GOLIAD FELL OCTOBER 9; THE BATTLE OF CONCEPCION WAS WON BY THE TEXANS, OCTOBER 28. SAN ANTONIO WAS CAPTURED DECEMBER 10, 1835 AFTER FIVE DAYS OF FIGHTING IN WHICH THE INDOMITABLE BENJAMIN R. MILAM DIED A HERO, AND THE MEXICAN ARMY EVACUATED TEXAS.

The Port of Houston Ship Channel above is lined on the north side by a series of wharves which have been specially constructed to handle the vast amount of cargo which daily passes in and out of the port. Equipment includes five gigantic cranes for dealing with container ships, such as the one shown above right, three powerful gantry cranes and a variety of mobile cranes.

The heavily industrialized area of the channel can be seen in daytime below, and at sunset overleaf.

Pictured left is the scene aboard the Inspection Vessel, Sam Houston, and right the floodlit Battleship Texas.

Night at the Opera

IN the center of Houston stands a rather severe, modern building with Greek undertones. Its simplicity is in keeping with the style of the contemporary city but it is also a reminder of the long line of Western cultural development that has taken place between the times of the Ancient Greeks and the present day. It is the Jesse H. Jones hall for the Performing Arts.

This elegant building is the home of the Houston Grand Opera Association and the Houston Symphony Orchestra and Ballet. During the season the courtyard in front of the Hall is crowded with opera-goers and music lovers moving about before the columns like the chorus in a Greek play and adding a colorful human touch to the geometric background.

The oldest of the performing arts to become established in Houston is music; the Houston Symphony Orchestra was founded in 1913 with thirty-five musicians – now ninety – supported by the same Miss Ima Hogg to whom Houston is indebted for the preservation of some fine examples of early American furniture and objets d'art at the Bayou Bend Museum. Although the concerts in Jones Hall are all subscribed to by loyal music lovers the orchestra also furthers the cause of music by giving free concerts in Hermann Park during the summer. Here in an open-air setting the Houston Symphony, which has been led by some of the world's most famous conductors including Sir John Barbirolli and Leopold Stokowski, plays to a large audience.

The musical life of Houston does not, however, depend on one orchestra; there are also the Houston Civic Symphony, the Houston Pops Orchestra and a youth symphony as well as various Chamber music groups, including those of the universities of Houston and St. Thomas.

Opera is also on the Houston musical program though the development of an international standard company has been as recent as 1972. John Vickers, Grace Bumby and Kostas Paskalis have all sung with the company which, like the Houston Symphony, performs at the Miller Theater in the summer months.

To complete the trio of traditional opera house entertainment there is the Houston Ballet which is considered among the top U.S. companies. The ballet program includes famous works such as the Nutcracker Suite and Swan Lake, as well as modern dance forms.

Drama is also well represented on the Houston evening scene. The Alley Theater is known far beyond the Texas borders and attracts top actors and actresses. The Alley is a modern complex which includes two theaters, the larger of which seats nearly 800 people and the smaller one 300. The foundation of the Alley Theater, which is downtown on Texas, is a romantic story of the enthusiasm of Nina Vance, who wrote to members of the Houston community in 1947 seeking their support for a Houston drama group. The reasons showed that a need existed and that there were plenty of people prepared to help fulfil it.

The present theater complex is the third in which the theater company has performed and its existence is due in large part to a generous grant by the Ford Foundaton which enabled the Alley Theater to erect a three-and-a-half-million-dollar building designed expressly for drama.

As with music the Houston enthusiasm for drama does not stop at the Alley Theater. The universities of Houston and St. Thomas both have drama departments and stage several shows a year. There are also several community theaters run and financed by private groups.

An original feature of Houston theater-going is that in many places the audience can eat dinner and watch the show, usually this is of the light comedy type or a musical. This all-in-one evening has grown in popularity, especially with the growing number of out-of-town visitors.

The high spots of the performing arts year are the summer concerts at Hermann Park. Here at Miller Theater with its shell roof stage the public can see and hear music, opera and musicals without charge. On the warm summer nights of Houston there is a vast cross-section of Houston society sitting in the park, informally dressed and provided with colorful blankets to sit on or with deck chairs for more comfort. Refreshments and food are part of the audience's equipment and the happy throng listening raptly to the music or talking or moving about animatedly during the intervals themselves add to the spectacle of Houston life under the summer stars.

Not quite on the same elevated plane as symphonies and opera but achieving the same dramatic qualities are the sports that Houstonians follow avidly, especially on summer evenings. The Astrodome, with its elaborate electronic equipment, is the sporting equivalent of Jones Hall and here in air-conditioned comfort the crowds cheer on their teams in the baseball games played during June, July and August.

There are nearly one hundred other lighted baseball diamonds in the city, so there is no lack of excitement for baseball fans, especially those who follow any one of the thirty-five teams that play in the league.

In winter there is football between teams that, with their heavy padding and helmets, look like martian invaders who struggle together like dinosaurs, in contrast there is the lithe grace of basketball players who keep the crowds on the edge of their seats at the Summit.

The beautiful interior of the Annunciation Church is illustrated left.

The exciting game of basketball was invented by an instructor in physical education at the International Young Men's Christian Association Training School (now Springfield College) Massachusetts, in 1891, and has since become one of the most famous national sports of the U.S. In the 20th century its popularity has increased enormously and this major sport is included in many international competitions, including the Olympic Games.

Houston's professional basketball team, the Rockets, were first introduced by the Texas Sports Investments in the early 1970's after they had finished the last season as the hottest team in the National Basketball Association, as the San Diego Rockets. Based at the Summit Stadium, the home team, in the red and white strip can be seen on these pages in an action-packed game with the visiting Blazers, and overleaf with the Bullets.

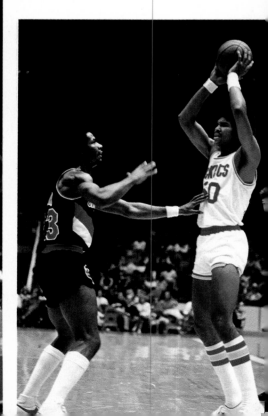

The superb Summit Stadium, in the Greenway Plaza above left, also serves as the home of Houston's hockey team, the Aeros, in addition to being the base for the Rockets. The Stadium is noted for its scrupulously clean, well-equipped rest rooms and bars and features opera seating and closed TV screens for slow-motion replays.

The basketball season lasts from October until April, with about three games being played each week, and the games are broadcast by the KPRC radio network.

Pictured right, below right and overleaf are further highlights from the game between the Rockets and the Bullets and below left between the Rockets and the Blazers.

The cheerleaders above and below are an integral part of most American sporting occasions and contribute glamor and entertainment for the spectators during the intervals.

After Dark

IKE all big cities with lively business centers and a constant flow of out-of-town visitors, Houston keeps going well into the night. Entertainment is found all over the city and ranges from the smart and sophisticated to the gimmicky and garish. In the large hotels there are the smooth , lowlit places that are the haven of the international traveler; elsewhere are the glittering watering holes where tired business people, and others less exhausted, can let their hair down and where the money flows almost as fast as the champagne.

In the early evening as the traffic goes speeding off along the freeways taking Houstonians back to their homes many people like to gather for a social drink in the lounges of the big hotels or in the bars along Westheimer. From many of the tall hotels like the Hyatt Regency there are spectacular panoramas of the prairie that stretches away in all directions beyond the residential area to the horizon.

After the cocktail·hour the restaurants spring to life and the variety and number of them – there are two thousand listed in the telephone book – is remarkable. Although the downtown area has a major concentration of eating places this is not, as in many conventional cities, the only place where one can get fine food.

The little cities within the big city, complexes like the Galleria, Greenway Plaza, to the west, Town and Country Village on Katy Freeway and other centers also have in and around them a choice of places offering a variety of international menus.

Those huge Texas steaks which are internationally famous can be found almost everywhere; two well recommended steak places are the Stables, downtown in Main Street and on Westheimer, and Brenner's on Katy Freeway.

Seafood is also something of a Houston speciality, some of the dishes originating in New Orleans. Gumbo is a rich spicy stew containing various kinds of seafood, Clam chowder is a clam soup richly flavored with herbs; and Bayou Bouillabaisse is the Houston version of the famous Marseillaise dish.

The New Orleans style with its nineteenth century French undertones is found at Courtlandt's a restaurant appropriately situated on Louisiana and furnished with the mirrors, crystal chandeliers and paneling of the period, and at Brennan's on Smith, which has retained the gaslight and curtained atmosphere in which Southern gentlemen and their belles conducted their romantic adventures.

Haute cuisine, though not a French monopoly is, nevertheless, primarily associated with French cooking and Houston has several restaurants where meals that would not be out of place in France can be enjoyed. Foulard's on Westheimer is one and Tony's at South Post Oak boasts many awards for its cuisine. Others are Le Pavillon at Post Oak Park and the Che, which despite its name specializes in French and Continental cuisine.

Though the French have acquired the reputation for fine food the Italians often claim that it was they who taught them the art when Maria de Medici married the French King Henry IV and took her Italian chefs to France. Whatever the truth of the story there is no doubt that Italian cooking is superb and the art is alive and well in Houston at such restaurants as Renata's on Lexington, where the vast menu is offered in a delightful ambience of hanging plants, awnings and skylights that give the illusion of being in Italy itself. Another typically Italian place is Michelangelo's on Westheimer, where one is surrounded by the Chianti bottles, bunches of grapes and other paraphernalia of an old-time Italian trattoria.

The Mexican tradition lingers on in Houston food with such dishes as tacos al carbon, a kind of pancake filled with charcoal-broiled lumps of beef, and chiles rellenos, stuffed peppers. Molina's Mexican City restaurants at Main and Westheimer are two of a chain that serves Mexican-Texan food and Marie's Tamale House is a small place with folk atmosphere. For the grand ambience the place to go is La Hacienda de los Morales on West Bolt Drive, a replica of an old Mexican hacienda with a Spanish colonial patio with massive stone buildings, fountains and high-ceilinged rooms, where Mexican and continental food is on the menu.

To go through the entire range of food available in Houston would take a book; suffice to say that the foods of all nations are available here with Chinese and Japanese food for people who enjoy the delicate flavors of the Orient and blinis and caviar at the Russian restaurant called Nikita. For more robust tastes there is Greek food at Zorba's, among others, and Polynesian food at Trader Vic's on Main Street.

Many of the restaurants combine entertainment with food and among these is Spindletop in the Hyatt Regency, where arrival in the restaurant is by means of a glass elevator which whisks one up the side of the building to the thirty-third floor where the revolving room allows diners a panoramic view of Houston while eating dinner. At the Savoy Room in the Houston Oaks Hotel there is dancing and six hours of entertainment and at Diamond Lil's Dining Emporium on West Loop one can dip into the atmosphere of Victorian America and dance in the legendary lady's saloon.

Among the sophisticated places with a smooth atmosphere is the Top of the Plaza in Greenway Plaza, from twenty stories up there is a fine night view of Houston as well as good cuisine. Dancing under the stars follows in the Plaza Suite Lounge on the same floor.

Two features of the Houston night scene are the Happy Hours, in the early evening when drinks are priced lower, and the piano bar, where one can drink to the accompaniment of mood inducing piano music.

The kind of shows that are designed for the international tourists are also part of the Houston night with topless bars, girlie shows and all the other titillations that are indispensable for the satisfaction of visitors from all parts of the world.

The lovely Fourth Church of Christ on Montrose Boulevard is shown left.

Spectacular Astroworld these pages and *overleaf provides fun and magic for all the family with a variety of extravaganzas, breathtaking roller coasters and fantastic firework displays.*

The Alabama-Coushatta Indian Reservation is located in the heart of the Sam Houston National Forest and is the largest Indian Reservation in Texas. Special attractions include a Museum, Arts and Craft shop, tribal dances, and tours through the Big Thicket Swamp. Amost 500 Indians live on the Reservation, maintaining the traditions and crafts of their ancestors, which can be seen in the Indian Village depicting life in the early 1800's.

Their colorful costumes and elaborate headdresses seen on these pages are particularly eye-catching, while right is shown an Indian skilfully shaping arrowheads in the traditional manner.

A Patron of the Arts

DESPITE the image of oilmen and Texas millionaires as a tough breed of men of action with little time for culture, few cities give as much support to the arts as Houston. Evidence of the interest in things of a cultural nature is seen at all levels of the community and much of this interest is no doubt due to the natural human desire for historical continuity which is especially acute among people who live in an environment without any visible links with the past.

The individual Houstonian evinces interest in the arts not only by support of the cultural institutions but on a personal level by collecting antiques and products of local craftsmanship. This interest has created an industry and antique and curio shops abound, as do craft shops where local pottery, glassware, jewelry and prints are on sale.

Much of the support for the cultural institutions has come about through individual patrons. Such is the case with the Bayou Bend Collection which is part of the Museum of Fine Arts. Bayou Bend was the home of Miss Ima Hogg, daughter of Governor and Mrs. James Hogg and was bequeathed to Houston by her. The Collection reflects Miss Hogg's lifelong interest in early American furniture and domestic articles and it provides a rare insight into the lives of the early pioneers and their struggle to maintain the niceties of life in a rough and unpropitious environment.

In another building of the Fine Arts Museum there is a good collection of the paintings of Remington who portrayed, in a romantic manner, the life of the westerner in the days of cattle ranching. His tough, scraggy horses loping along the prairie or swirling in a cloud of dust as they round up the cattle present a vivid picture of the solitary and arduous life of the cowboys.

The American past is also preserved by the Heritage Society, which is responsible for the restoration of some of Houston's few old buildings. These lie downtown amid the rush and bustle of freeway traffic and include a Texas house of 1847, the year the first railway was established in the State with the name of Buffalo Bayou, Brazos and Colorado Railway. There is also a wooden cabin of the type built by early settlers, a church and some cottages. To add to the sense of the past the Society has also preserved some lamp-posts and benches which formerly lined the Houston streets.

The ephemera of everyday life is preserved at the Museum of American Architecture and Decorative Arts, where there is a collection of household utensils, toys and dolls as well as furniture and silverware. This small but interesting collection is at the Library, Houston Baptist University.

Among the most fascinating of the large museums is the Museum of Natural Sciences, and Medical Sciences. As well as containing the usual exhibits of paleontological interest, the Natural Science Museum includes a Hall of Petroleum Science, which is very appropriate for a city whose wealth comes from this natural resource, and a Hall of the American Indian, which features among others, the Indians of the Karankawa tribes who lived along the coastal plains before the arrival of the white man. Inevitable in a city in which space exploration is almost equal in importance to the energy business, there is a Hall of Space Science and a Planetarium, where the public can look through the sixteen inch Mary Root Brown telescope, the largest in the Houston area.

Historically the most important museum area is at San Jacinto, reached by driving east through the petrochemical industrial center, where markers on the battleground tell the story of the fateful encounter between the Texans headed by Sam Houston and the Mexicans under Santa Ana. Oak woods, ponds and picnic sites are features of the area and there is a monument dedicated to those who won independence for Texas. The monument is a column 570 feet high topped by the symbol of the lone star state; an elevator takes visitors to the top of the column under the star. Nearby is the battleship Texas II which saw action at Okinawa and Normandy and can now be visited; a last reminder of the days when naval power was the key to world power.

Though the past is of absorbing interest to Houstonians the nature of their community is such that the experimental and exploratory forms of art are equally if not more important to them. In the Contemporary Arts Museum there are constantly changing exhibitions of paintings and sculptures by modern masters; these are housed in a steel parallelogram that expresses the spirit of the Museum. For those who prefer a more traditional approach to art there is the Museum of Fine Arts which, as well as presenting the masters of the Renaissance, also arranges special exhibitions of famous modern masters like Paul Cézanne and the painters of the School of Paris.

The most significant and complete modern art exhibit in Houston is the Rothko Chapel. Here the vast brooding canvases with their flat, formless surfaces create a mood, in the same way as Monet's famous pond pictures, but in this case there are no points of reference to lead the mind to a tangible and recognizable reality.

The skyscrapers of Downtown Houston left rise from the prairie land of southwest America and help to form this, the nation's sixth largest city.

...elieved to be the oldest remaining structure in ...arris County, the 'Old Place' center right was ...iginally built on a hill on the west side of Clear ...reek, and is though to date back to the ...id-1820's. Despite considerable alterations ...roughout the years much of the original fabric of ...e cabin has remained and with further ...storation work now completed it is preserved in ...e Sam Houston Park. The simply furnished ...terior of the building can be seen above left.

...he Nichols-Rice-Cherry House above was ...iginally built on the corner of San Jacinto and ...ongress Avenues in about 1850. Acquired by the ...arris County Heritage Society in 1959, it was ...ismantled and moved to Sam Houston Park ...here it was carefully reconstructed. Its ...aditionally furnished kitchen is shown below ...ft.

...onstructed in 1868, the Pillot House top right is ... symmetrical Victorian cottage revealing the ...Eastlake' influence, and was built by Eugene ...illot whose family had emigrated to America ...om France in 1832. One of the delightful ...arlors of this single story house is pictured ...ottom right.

...evealing its clear and simple lines, St John ...Church below, came into being about 1891 in the ...German farming community of White Oak in ...orthwest Harris County. Moved to Sam ...Iouston Park in 1968, the belfry and octagonal ...eeple are considered to be the church's most ...utstanding exterior feature.

Part of the Museum of Fine Arts, Bayou Bend on Westcott Street is a gracious 1928 mansion which houses a superb collection of 17th, 18th and early 19th century American antiques. The former home of the late Miss Ima Hogg, daughter of the first native-born governor of Texas, the house is set adjacent to Memorial Park on Buffalo Bayou, amid an elaborate garden setting.

The beautifully furnished rooms illustrated on these pages are part of twenty-four rooms of American furniture which show the exquisite craftsmanship from the time of the Pilgrim era to the mid-Victorian period.

The magnificent Harris County Domed Stadium, known as the Astrodome these pages and overleaf, is the world's first enclosed, air-conditioned major league baseball stadium.
Standing on a 260-acre site the stadium has a plush seating capacity for up to 66,000 people and boasts the world's largest electronic scoreboard.

Home of the Houston Astro's, the team is featured on these pages in a stimulating game against the Giants.

Houston's modern buildings are reflected in the facade of the Coastal Tower left, and below can be seen the glittering fountain in Memorial Park.

With a collection of exhibits spanning over 5,000 years the Museum of Fine Arts contains some of the finest examples of world art. The sculptures above are set in the Museum's delightful grounds.

The dinosaur exhibit above right, a reconstructed Diplodocus skeleton measuring feet in length and dating back 160 million years, is one of the exciting displays on view in the Museum of Natural Science.

Houston's Zoological Gardens provide naturalistic environments for the many rare species, such as the gorilla shown below right, which inhabit this unique zoo.

A host of star-spangled banners flutter outside the Summit Stadium overleaf.

First published in Great Britain 1979 by Colour Library International Ltd.
© Illustrations: Colour Library International Ltd., 163 East 64th St., New York, N.Y. 10021.
Colour separations by Fercrom, Barcelona, Spain.
Display and text filmsetting by Focus Photoset, London, England.
Printed and bound by SAGDOS - Brugherio (MI), Italy.
All rights reserved.
ISBN 0-8317-4592-4 Library of Congress Catalogue Card No. 79-2125
Published in the United States of America by Mayflower Books, Inc., New York City
Published in Canada by Wm. Collins and Sons, Toronto